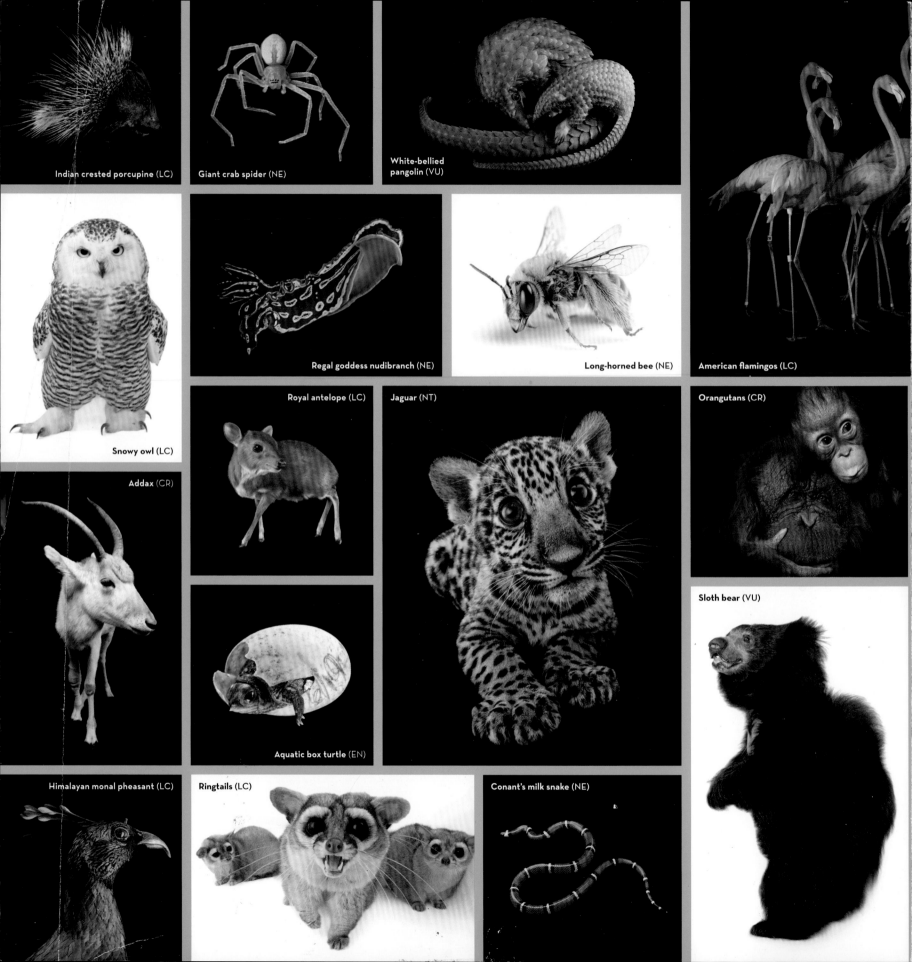

Indian crested porcupine (LC)

Giant crab spider (NE)

White-bellied pangolin (VU)

Snowy owl (LC)

Regal goddess nudibranch (NE)

Long-horned bee (NE)

American flamingos (LC)

Addax (CR)

Royal antelope (LC)

Jaguar (NT)

Orangutans (CR)

Aquatic box turtle (EN)

Sloth bear (VU)

Himalayan monal pheasant (LC)

Ringtails (LC)

Conant's milk snake (NE)

Rabbs' fringe-limbed tree frog (CR)

Keel-billed toucan (LC)

Suwannee moccasinshell (CR)

Tortoise beetle (NE)

Reticulated giraffe (LC)

Lined seahorse (VU)

Koalas (VU)

Pink sponge (NE)

Madagascar giant day gecko (LC)

Siamese fighting fish (VU)

Indian rhinoceroses (VU)

Radiated tortoise (CR)

Black-footed ferret (EN)

AnimalArk

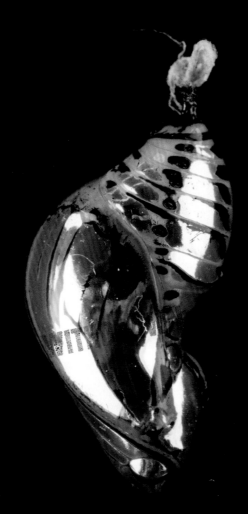

Celebrating our
WILD WORLD
in **poetry**
and **pictures**

NATIONAL GEOGRAPHIC

PHOTOARK
JOEL SARTORE

Photographs by **JOEL SARTORE,** Photo Ark Creator

Words by **KWAME ALEXANDER,** Winner of the Newbery Medal

With Mary Rand Hess and Deanna Nikaido

NATIONAL GEOGRAPHIC
Washington, D.C.

chorus of **creatures**

singing our names

see what we can save—**together**

look into these **eyes**

full of **secret**

places to **hide**

and

play

a feathered **rainbow dance**

curiosity that **LEAPS**

homes of courage

on **humble backs** this is **not a race**

embracing **wonder**

SLIDING and GLIDING

waiting for you to notice

spots blend **unseen**

so they can **STALK**, swim

sneak up on us

listen to the rumble

giant stomping feet

calling brothers ... sisters

blink and you'll miss
the hush of waves, **tiny** feet
scurrying inside dunes

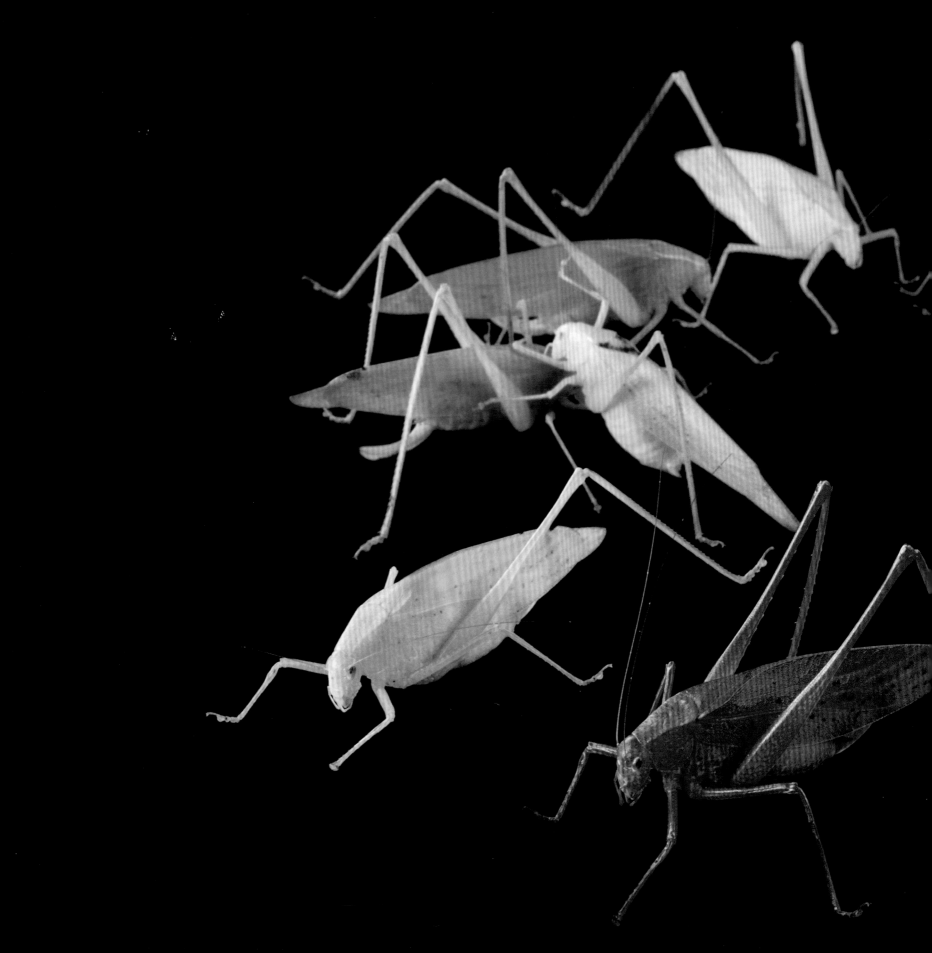

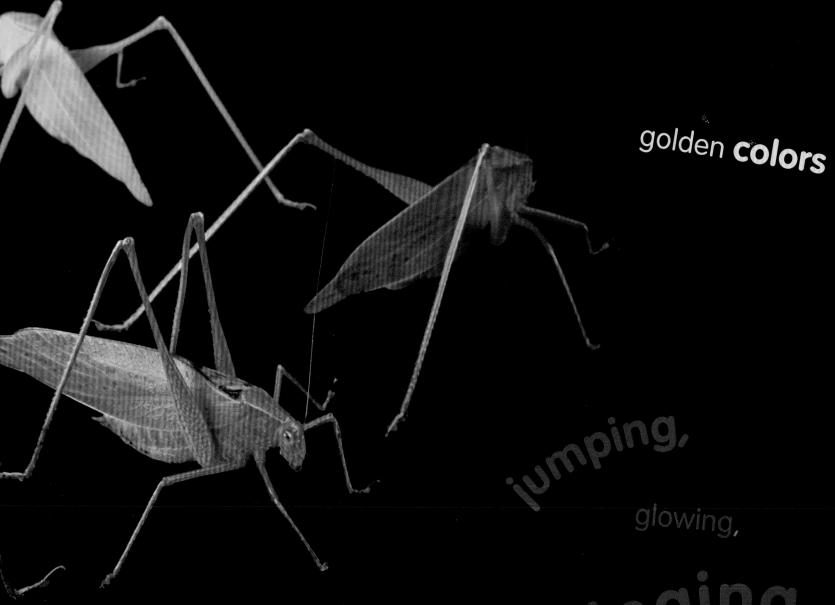

enchanting electric

golden **colors**

jumping,

glowing,

singing

wings like a **cape,**
ready for **flight**

into the sweet, **dark night**

how many **feathers** . . . does it take to make a **wing**

Diablito (NT)

American great egret (LC)

African moon moth (NE)

Rowley's palm pit viper (VU)

White-headed vulture (CR)

Snow leopard (EN)

Blue-eyed black lemur (CR)

Damaraland mole rat (LC)

Grevy's zebra (EN)

Spotted jellyfish (NE)

Spanish shawl nudibranch (NE)

Macaroni penguin (VU)

Western lowland gorilla (CR)

Red pandas (EN)

Arizona tiger salamander (LC)

Butterfly splitfin (EW)

Chorus of Creatures

WE ARE FAMILY. **Miraculous each.** The strangely inquisitive and the dangerously direct. Some nearly invisible with oversized zest. **Breathing one sky. Forever connected** by this peculiar and wonderful family tree. Branches that soar, swim, stalk. **Butterflies, turtles, leopards.**

Do you remember?

Close your eyes tight. We are all made of light. Some of us even glow. We are **secret siblings.** Reflections of each other. Mysterious mirrors.

Stand up. Stand out.

Respect the viper and the beetle. The fox and the tiger. The majestic and powerful are **counting on us to help them.**

WILD at heart

with slow, measured moves

and eyes **BIG** as **two sunsets**

TO FLY, SHARE SKY

Pacific blood star (NE)

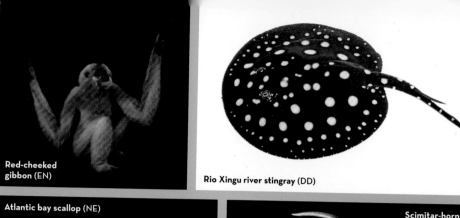

Red-cheeked gibbon (EN)

Rio Xingu river stingray (DD)

Northern blue-tongued skink (NE)

Atlantic bay scallop (NE)

Scimitar-horned oryx (EW)

Orange-bellied parrot (CR)

Galápagos tortoise (VU)

Arctic fox (LC)

Yellow-striped caecilian (LC)

Harlequin frog (NE)

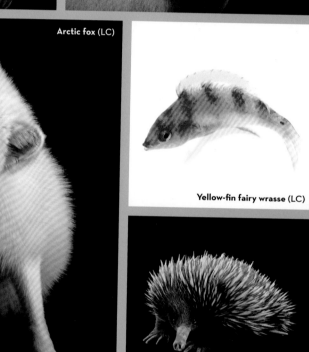

Yellow-fin fairy wrasse (LC)

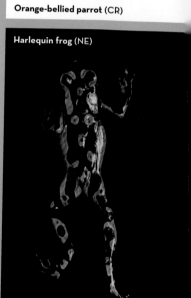

Kangaroo Island echidna (LC)

Beluga sturgeon (CR)

Reddish parachute spider (EN)

Virginia opossums (LC)

Fossa (VU)

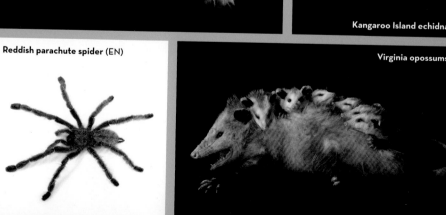

There are **too few remaining**

in the **rain forest**
in the **big blue sea**
in the whole wide world

because of you and me.

Our actions matter. They reach to the smallest of us. And the biggest. Remember, **we are part of forever.** Zipping and zooming and diving and dashing from place to space. **Angels with fins** and **iridescent armies** on the move. Blending for protection. Blending with the moon. Nature is genius. This is our home.

Listen. **We are unique. We share a story.** A beginning, a middle, and if we are not careful ... an end.

Let us take care of our home. Stones and ripples both. There are thousands and thousands of stars above us **holding our wishes,** and coming true takes time. But we must move quickly, family. **Pay this friendship forward.** Watch out for each other—the cool, calm, and cuddly. Listen to the earth. That sound you hear is **hope with wings.**

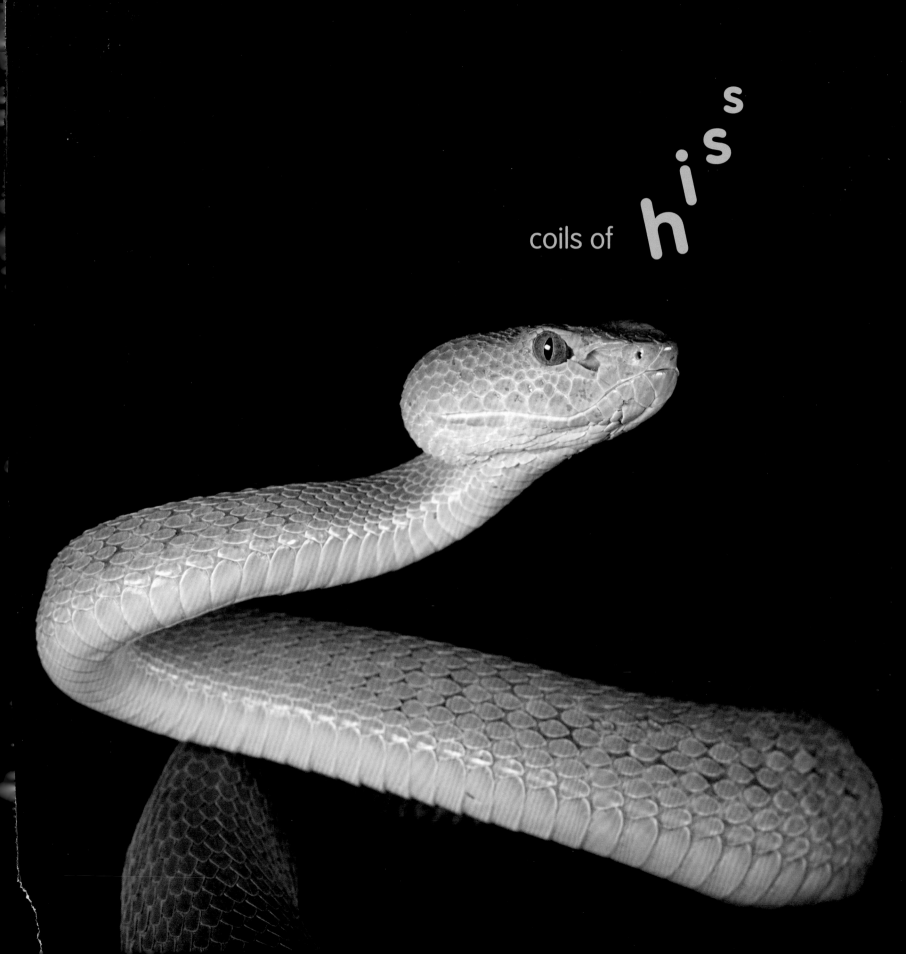

coils of hⁱ^s^s

A Note From the Photographer

At its heart, the Photo Ark was born out of necessity.

I have been sent around the world by *National Geographic* magazine for more than 20 years to take photographs of people, places, and animals. There have been assignments to capture images of the fiercest predators, the shyest sea creatures, the most beautiful birds, and so many more. Several years ago, I started to see that people weren't paying much attention to the fate of all the other species we share this planet with. Without action, and soon, I worried that many animals could go extinct.

The Photo Ark is my answer to this. By introducing the entire world to thousands of photographs of mammals, birds, reptiles, amphibians, fish, and even insects, I hope we can get everyone following, liking, texting, tweeting, and even talking about this wondrous world of ours.

In the Photo Ark, every creature is equal. I use simple black and white backgrounds, which make all animals appear to be the same size, no matter how large or small they might be in the wild. Each photo also shows you the amazing detail of a creature's scales, skin, or feathers; their eyes, antennae, or legs—each creature with its own kind of stunning beauty. A slippery minnow in the Photo Ark appears as big as a shark, and a tiny tiger beetle as impressive as a mighty tiger.

I want people around the world to look these animals in the eye, and then fall in love with creatures as dazzling as a pheasant or as odd as an octopus. And once we love something, won't we do anything to save it?

So just how can you get started saving species? There are many ways—and it starts by protecting our planet. Defend animal ecosystems by reducing, reusing, and recycling every product you can. Think sustainably, knowing that whatever you buy is made somewhere and out of something. Ask yourself: Is it good for the planet? And talk to your family about becoming a member of your local zoo or aquarium. They're the real arks now, working hard every day to save everything from aardvarks to zebras.

I believe all of us have a great capacity to care. And when we do, we can accomplish amazing things. I've seen it with my own eyes many times: The wildlife rehabilitator who opens her home to treat injured small mammals; the private breeder who works for years to save critically endangered birds; or the teacher who shares his love of butterflies with generations of children.

All are environmental heroes to me. You can be one too, if you just look around, and care.

Now, what will you do to make this world a better place?

—*Joel Sartore*

The National Geographic Photo Ark is a multiyear effort with photographer Joel Sartore to photograph every captive species to inspire people to save those most vulnerable, while also funding conservation projects focused on those in most critical need of protection.

grandfather of the **hunt**

FIERCE and **FAST**

and **favored,** forever?

strong, yet **gentle** . . . **black** and **white**

championing human nature

spooky **webs** spinning

a **deadly** tattoo:

STAY AWAY!

a **hundred feet**

walking without a sound

one direction

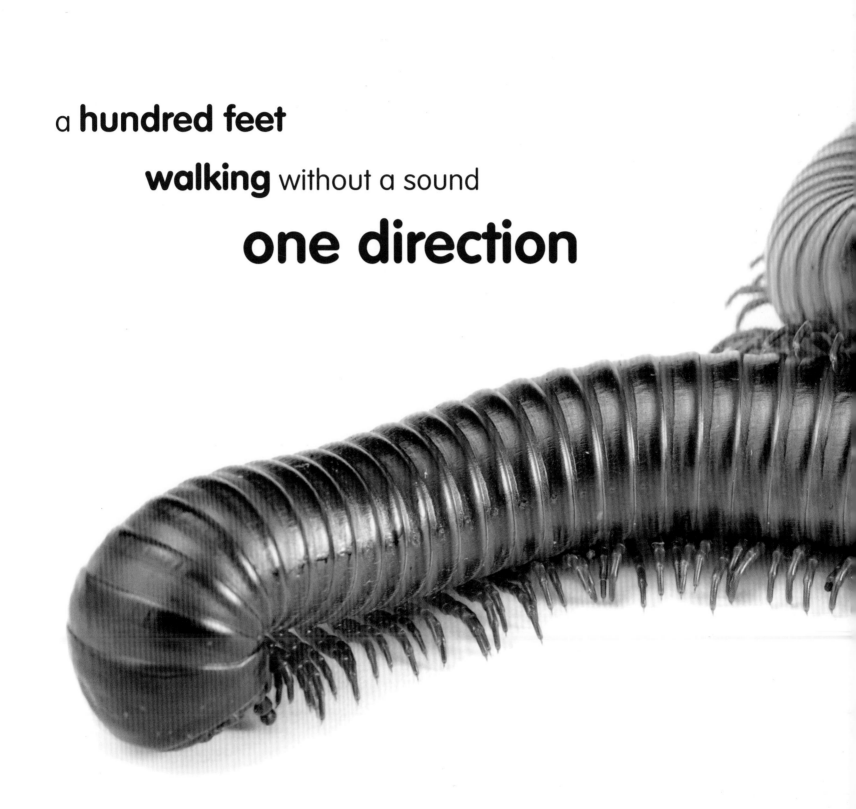

tiny growls

new to the chase

innocent wander

a thousand silent waving arms

GRAB HOLD OF US!

a pair of **claws**

HOWL

like you mean it . . . the world is **listening**

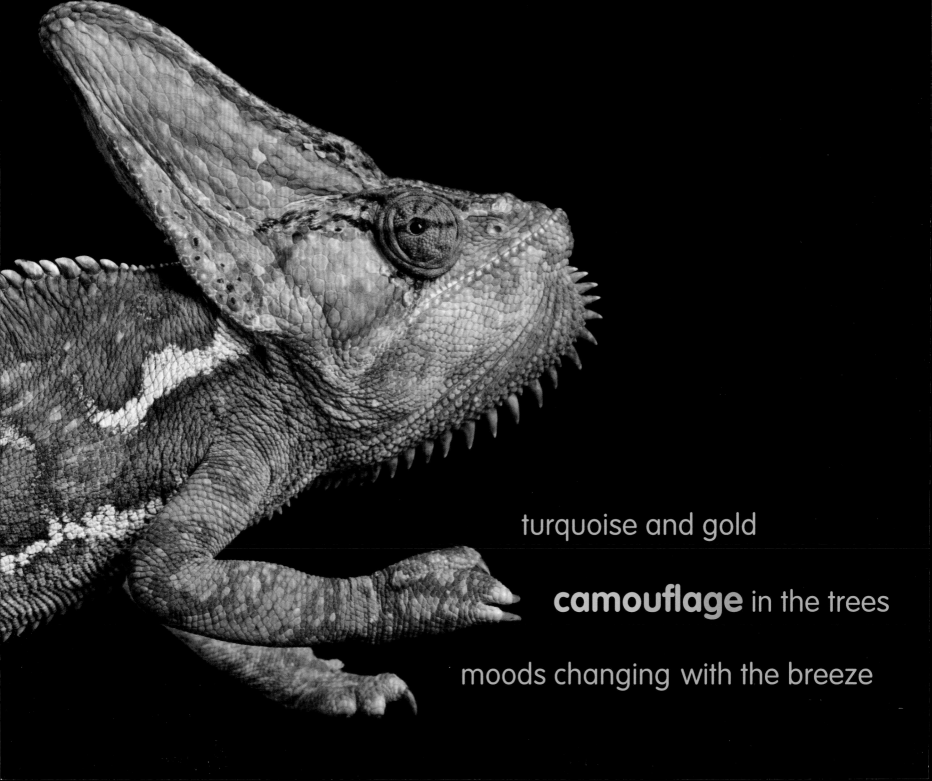

turquoise and gold

camouflage in the trees

moods changing with the breeze

color me **ANCIENT** and **SACRED**

from **glistening sea**

to **rising sun**

Mohawk **plume** . . . . sharp, stinging **beauty**

To Cole, Ellen, and Spencer —JS

For Ann Marie, champion of the wild —KA

For Ronnie and Betsy, my first storytellers —MRH

For Landon and Nicholas, live what you love —DN

Text Copyright © 2017 Kwame Alexander
Photographs Copyright © 2017 Joel Sartore
Compilation Copyright © 2017 National Geographic Partners, LLC

The publisher would like to thank everyone who made this book possible: Kate Hale, senior editor; Lori Epstein, director of photography; Amanda Larsen, design director; Paige Towler, associate editor; and Joan Gossett, editorial production manager.

Special thanks also to the team who support the Photo Ark and who have been an invaluable help on this book: Colby Bishop, program manager; Pierre de Chabannes, scientific adviser; Maura Mulvihill, program director; and Rebecca Wright, office manager at Joel Sartore Photography.

Since 1888, the National Geographic Society has funded more than 12,000 research, exploration, and preservation projects around the world. The Society receives funds from National Geographic Partners LLC, funded in part by your purchase. A portion of the proceeds from this book supports this vital work.

For more information, visit www.natgeo.com/info, call 1-800-647-5463, or write to the following address:
National Geographic Partners
1145 17th Street N.W.
Washington, D.C. 20036-4688 U.S.A.

Visit us online at nationalgeographic.com/books

For librarians and teachers: ngchildrensbooks.org
More for kids from National Geographic: kids.nationalgeographic.com

For information about special discounts for bulk purchases, please contact National Geographic Books Special Sales: specialsales@natgeo.com

For rights or permissions inquiries, please contact National Geographic Books Subsidiary Rights: bookrights@natgeo.com

NATIONAL GEOGRAPHIC and Yellow Border Design are trademarks of the National Geographic Society, used under license.

Designed by Amanda Larsen

Hardcover ISBN: 978-1-4263-2767-4
Library Binding ISBN: 978-1-4263-2768-1

Printed in China
16/RRDS/1

Brown-throated sloth
LC
Parts of Central
and South America

**Eastern tiger
swallowtail butterfly**
NE
Eastern
North America

Giant rainforest mantis
NE
Australia

**Feather-tailed
centipede**
NE
Eastern Africa

**Red celestial eye
goldfish**
LC
Parts of Asia

**Cream-spotted
tigerwing butterfly
chrysalis**
NE
Parts of Central
and South America

**Pearl Charaxes
butterfly**
NE
Africa

**Common lime
butterfly**
NE
Australia and
southeastern Asia

Waxy monkey frog
LC
Parts of
South America

Ploughshare tortoises
CR
Madagascar

Coquerel's sifaka
EN
Madagascar

American alligator
LC
Southeastern
United States

African leopard
VU
Parts of Africa

Bobtail squid
DD
Coastal waters
in Pacific Ocean
and Indian Ocean

Asian elephant
EN
Southeastern Asia

Green jay
LC
Parts of North, Central,
and South America

Pope's tree viper
NE
Southeastern Asia

Guianan cock-of-the-rock
LC
Northern
South America

Two-spined angelfish
LC
Coastal waters in
Pacific Ocean and
Indian Ocean

Darkling beetle
NE
Worldwide

**Notch-mouthed
ground beetle**
NE
Parts of North
and Central America

**Derbyana
flower beetle**
NE
Parts of Africa

Clouded leopard
VU
Southeastern Asia

Asian millipede
NE
Tropical regions worldwide

Southern black widow
NE
Parts of the
United States

Giant panda cubs
EN
Central China

Malayan tiger
CR
Malay Peninsula
in southeastern Asia

Rainbow scarab
NE
Parts of the
United States

Mexican bluewing butterfly
NE
Parts of North and Central America

Tiger longwing butterfly
NE
Parts of Central and South America

Gulf fritillary butterfly
NE
Parts of North, Central, and South America

Malachite butterfly
NE
Parts of North, Central, and South America

Common green birdwing butterfly
NE
Parts of Asia, Australia, and Oceania

Great southern white butterfly
NE
Parts of North, Central, and South America

Mandrill
VU
Western Africa

Red-crested turaco
LC
Western Africa

St. Andrew beach mouse
EN
Southeastern United States

Oblong-winged katydids
NE
Parts of North America

Lesser short-nosed fruit bat
LC
Southeastern Asia

Bengal slow loris
VU
Southeastern Asia

Blue waxbills
LC
Parts of Africa

Northern tamandua
LC
Parts of Central and South America

Emerald beetle
NE
Eastern Africa

Milkweed leaf beetle
NE
Parts of North America

Veiled chameleon
LC
Arabian Peninsula in western Asia

Mexican gray wolf
LC
Southeastern United States and Northern Mexico

Common yabby
VU
Australian freshwater

Variegated sea urchin
NE
Tropical waters in western Atlantic Ocean

Malayan tapir
EN
Southeastern Asia

Quokka
VU
Southwestern Australia

Chimpanzee
EN
Parts of Africa

About IUCN Listings

The International Union for Conservation of Nature and Natural Resources (IUCN) is a global group dedicated to sustainability. The IUCN Red List of Threatened Species is a comprehensive collection of animal and plant species that have been analyzed according to their risk of extinction. Once evaluated, a species is placed into one of several categories. Each species' current IUCN status is listed alongside its name and where it can be found in the wild.

EX: Extinct
EW: Extinct in the wild
CR: Critically endangered
EN: Endangered
VU: Vulnerable
NT: Near threatened
LC: Least concern
DD: Data Deficient
NE: Not evaluated

A Note From the Writer

Lately I have been drawn to collaborative projects. Part of it is I seem to have more ideas these days, and less time to implement them alone. But, also, I love the tremendous feeling of being connected to like-minded artists who inspire me. Who encourage me to become better. As a poet. As a man. As a human being. It is that same feeling of connectedness and humanity that brought me and my dear writerly friends, Deanna and Mary, to *Animal Ark* and the incredible artistic preservation of Joel Sartore.

Speaking of poetry, this project resonated with me as a writer because of the parallel nature between powerful photographs and poetry as narrative—which is in its own way a kind of literary snapshot. Both have the ability to bypass the skin and enter through the heart, transforming what is often difficult to convey into something universal.

I wondered how to approach the subject matter of endangered animals with children like my own eight-year-old daughter, who has many questions, and who is more aware of things than I sometimes give her credit for. How would I bring forth a visual conversation, full of rhythm and imagery and movement and conciseness that plants seeds so she knows they need watering? Even more, how would my page live up to the majestic and magical stage that Joel has presented to us so lovely?

After working with hundreds of students of all ages, I have found when using the Japanese form of haiku that something about its brevity creates an instant connection.

The more sparse and condensed the language is, the more potent the message. Joel Sartore's photographs are exquisite visual haiku that capture something even words cannot, and yet the combination of the two creates a landscape, a third language only the heart knows. Thirty-two of these precious animals are given special attention in this book, but there are thousands more. My hope, and Mary's prayer, and Deanna's belief is that this is only the beginning of the many ways in which we can address this home we all share, whether human or animal. Change can begin with a thought; a conversation; a photograph; a poem.

—*Kwame Alexander*

Haiku

Traditional Japanese haiku is a seventeen-syllable, three-line poem—where the first line has five syllables, the second line has seven, and the third has five. Known for its concentrated brevity and reference to nature, it can sometimes vary in syllables and theme due to cultural and untranslatable differences in language (consider the word "haiku" itself has two syllables in English and three in Japanese). In any language, the beauty of this poetry form is in its concise power, and its ability to frame in some abstract way a complete thought with the subtle qualities of a question. It's the perfect complement to these incredible photographs. Both should inspire continued conversation. Look at the images in *Animal Ark* and try creating your own haiku!